Contents Guide

Welcome & What You'll Learn

Welcome to the exciting world of Git and GitHub! As a software developer—whether you're a seasoned pro or just starting your coding adventures—you've likely heard about these powerful tools. Perhaps you've even taken a few tentative steps into their realm. If so, you're in the right place! This book is your comprehensive guide to mastering the essentials of Git and GitHub, propelling you towards version control mastery and collaborative development success.

Let's break down what's in store for you!

What exactly is Git?

At its core, Git is a distributed version control system (DVCS). Picture it as a remarkably clever time machine for your code. It allows you to:

- **Snapshots of your project:** Git lets you take snapshots of your codebase at crucial moments, called "commits".
- **Travel back in time:** Feeling nostalgic for a past version of your code? Git lets you rewind the clock and revisit earlier stages of your project.
- **Experiment freely:** Git encourages exploration by introducing the concept of "branches." These are like parallel universes where you can test new features or try out wild ideas without messing up your main codebase.

Why should you care about Git?

Git is a game-changer, and here's why:

- **Safety Net:** Made a huge coding blunder? Git lets you roll back changes and recover from missteps with ease.
- **Collaboration Powerhouse:** Git facilitates seamless teamwork. Multiple developers can work on the same project simultaneously, track changes, and merge code without breaking things.

- **Time Travel:** Need to reference an older (and hopefully bug-free) version of your project? Git stores your entire code history for easy access.
- **Industry Standard:** Git is embraced by tech companies and open-source communities around the world. Mastering it makes you a more valuable and adaptable developer.

Enter GitHub

Think of GitHub as a cloud-based home for your Git projects. It's a platform where you can:

- **Store your code remotely:** A safe haven for your precious code, protected from accidental coffee spills and hard drive failures.
- **Collaborate effortlessly:** GitHub fosters teamwork, allowing you to invite others to work on your projects, make suggestions, and resolve conflicts smoothly.
- **Showcase your work:** GitHub acts as a portfolio for your coding creations, visible to potential employers and fellow developers.
- **Connect with the community:** Discover thousands of open-source projects, learn from others, and even contribute to the massive world of shared code.

What You'll Gain from This Book

Embarking on this Git and GitHub journey will equip you with essential skills vital for any modern software developer. By the end of this book, you will be able to:

- **Manage your code with confidence:** Control the flow of your project's evolution, safeguarding your hard work and tracking every change.
- **Collaborate like a pro:** Work harmoniously with other developers, merging code efficiently and contributing effectively to team projects.
- **Leverage the power of the GitHub community:** Find inspiration, learn from the best, and give back by sharing your own knowledge.
- **Enhance your development workflow:** Streamline your coding processes, saving time and minimizing frustration.

If you're a developer wanting to level up your skills, Git and GitHub are non-negotiable. This book is your all-inclusive guide. Let's dive into the fascinating world of version control and open-source collaboration!

Are you ready for this transformation?

Let's get started!

Section 1:
Laying the Groundwork

Unveiling Git: Unleash Your Development Potential

Imagine you're writing a thrilling novel. You work tirelessly on a fantastic chapter, but halfway through, something goes terribly wrong. Perhaps you accidentally delete a pivotal scene or introduce a major plot hole. Without a backup, your hard work could vanish in an instant. Ouch!

Now, think about software development. Projects involve hundreds, sometimes thousands, of lines of code delicately woven together. A minor change or an unforeseen bug can unravel the whole intricate tapestry you've created. That's where Git enters the scene as your coding superhero!

What exactly is Git?

Git is a distributed version control system (DVCS). This may sound complex, but let's break it down:

- **Version Control:** Git is like a meticulous photographer for your code. It constantly takes snapshots of your project at different development stages. If things go awry, you can easily travel back in time and restore your project to a previous, functional state.
- **Distributed:** Unlike traditional centralized version control systems, Git doesn't rely on a single central server. Every developer has a complete copy (or clone) of the entire project's history on their local machine. This means you can work offline, experiment freely, and collaborate without constantly needing an internet connection.

Why Git Matters: The Superpowers it Grants Developers

1. **A Fearless Safety Net:** Experimentation is the fuel of innovation. Git empowers you to try new ideas, add features, and refactor your

code without the paralyzing fear of breaking everything irrevocably. If things go south, you can always roll back to a working version.

2. **Non-Linear Development:** Git introduces the concept of "branches." Imagine your project as a tree trunk. Branches are like alternate timelines where you can test features, fix bugs, and explore different paths without affecting the main trunk (your stable codebase).

3. **The Time Travel Advantage:** Ever wanted to revisit older versions of your code? Perhaps you need to compare your current work to a past implementation or pinpoint when a particular bug sneaked in. Git's time machine has your back!

4. **Effortless Collaboration:** Modern software development is almost always a team effort. Git is designed from the ground up to facilitate collaboration. Developers can work on their branches and then seamlessly merge their changes into the main project while carefully managing any conflicts that may arise.

5. **Project Transparency:** Git keeps a meticulous change log. Who changed what, when, and why? This clear history offers valuable insights into the evolution of your codebase, making it easier to track bugs, understand decisions, and maintain your project over time.

Git in the Real World

Git has revolutionized the way software is built. Let's look at some scenarios where it shines:

- **Open-Source Software:** Projects like Linux (the backbone of Android and countless servers) are powered by Git. Thousands of developers worldwide contribute to such open-source projects, and Git elegantly orchestrates this collaborative dance.
- **Web Development Teams:** Teams building complex websites and applications rely on Git to manage the contributions of multiple developers, designers, and content writers.
- **Individual Game Developers:** Even solo developers find Git indispensable for experimenting, tracking progress, and maintaining different versions of their games.

Git + GitHub: A Powerful Duo

While Git is phenomenal as a local version control tool, its true power gets amplified when paired with GitHub. GitHub is a cloud-based platform built around Git. It provides:

- **Secure Off-site Storage:** Safeguard your code on GitHub's servers, shielded from accidental deletions or hardware failures on your local machine.
- **Centralized Hub for Collaboration:** GitHub invites you to a global community of developers, encouraging teamwork and code sharing.
- **Professional Portfolio:** Showcase your coding skills for potential employers and collaborators.

Let's Get Started!

Are you ready to transform the way you develop software? Git is an essential tool for modern developers of all levels. In the upcoming chapters, we'll dive deeper and get hands-on with Git's core concepts and commands.

Additional Resources

- **Git's Official Documentation:** https://git-scm.com/doc

Buckle up and get ready to unleash the potential of Git!

Navigating Git's Terrain: Your Path to Version Control Mastery

In the previous chapter, we unveiled Git and its development-transforming superpowers. Now, it's time to chart your journey through Git's conceptual landscape. Understanding these fundamental concepts lays a rock-solid foundation upon which you'll build your practical Git skills in subsequent chapters.

Key Concepts to Master

Let's explore some of the core principles that make Git tick:

1. **Repositories:** A Git repository (or "repo" for short) is the heart of a Git-managed project. Consider it a grand archive that houses your entire codebase, along with its complete history. Repositories can exist locally on your computer (local repository) or remotely on platforms like GitHub (remote repository).
2. **Commits:** Think of commits as the milestones on your project's timeline. Each commit captures a snapshot of your code at a specific moment. Commits must always include a message succinctly describing the changes made. Good commit messages are vital for understanding your project's history.
3. **Branches:** Branches are like parallel development tracks within your project. The default branch is typically called "main" or "master." You can create new branches to safely develop new features or experiment without affecting your main, stable codebase. Once a feature is ready, you merge those changes seamlessly back into the main branch.
4. **Staging Area:** This is a temporary holding place where you meticulously prepare the changes you want to include in your next commit. The staging area lets you selectively add files or even specific changes within files, ensuring fine-grained control over your commits.
5. **Snapshots, not Differences:** Git is clever. Unlike some older version control systems, instead of just tracking file differences, it takes entire snapshots of your project at each commit point. This

approach empowers efficient storage and makes it lightning-fast to navigate your history.

6. **The Magic of Three: Working Tree, Staging Area, and Repository**

Understanding the interplay between these three crucial areas is key to grasping Git's workflow:

- **Working Tree:** This is where your active code lives—the files and folders you directly interact with in your code editor.
- **Staging Area:** Files and changes you intend to commit are assembled here for review before they're officially sealed into history.
- **Repository:** The repository is your project's grand historical record, safely storing each commit with its snapshot, message, author, and timestamp.

A Typical Git Workflow (Simplified)

Let's outline the general steps involved when using Git:

1. **Modify your code:** Work on your project's files in your working tree, adding, editing, and deleting code as needed.
2. **Stage changes:** Use Git commands to selectively add modified files or specific portions of files to the staging area.
3. **Commit the changes:** Create a new commit, encompassing the staged changes. Include a clear and concise commit message.
4. **Push to a remote repository (optional):** If you're working with a remote repository on a platform like GitHub, you can 'push' your commits to share your work and collaborate.
5. **Pull from a remote repository (optional):** Retrieve changes ('pull') made by others from the remote repository and update your local copy.

The Non-Linear Beauty

Remember, Git's distributed nature and branching system let you hop between commits, rewind to past states, explore alternative development paths, and then gracefully merge your changes together. This non-linear workflow gives you unprecedented freedom in software development!

Visualization Tools

Conceptualizing Git's structure is much easier with visual aids. Many resources and tools help you visualize repositories, branches, and commits. Here is the one to check out:

- **Learn Git Branching:** https://learngitbranching.js.org/ (Interactive visual playground)

Getting Ready for Hands-On Practice

Theory is essential, but the true magic of Git unfolds through practice. In the upcoming chapters, we'll install Git, set up a GitHub account, and dive into using Git commands to manage your code like a seasoned pro.

Additional Resources

- **Git Cheat Sheet:** A concise command reference (https://training.github.com/downloads/github-git-cheat-sheet/)

Let's continue forging your path toward Git mastery!

Initiating Git and GitHub: Embarking on Your Coding Journey

It's time to take your first practical steps in the realm of Git and GitHub! In this chapter, we'll cover the essentials:

- **Setting up Git on your system:** Ensuring Git is installed and configured correctly.
- **Creating your GitHub account:** Joining the global developer community.
- **Initializing your first project with Git:** Bringing your first project under Git's watchful eye.

Step 1: Installing Git & Configuring Your Environment

Installation processes vary slightly depending on your operating system. Here's the gist, but we'll provide links to detailed instructions:

- **macOS:** Most likely, Git is already installed. You can check by opening the Terminal and typing `git --version`. If not installed, consider using a package manager like Homebrew (https://brew.sh/) or downloading the installer directly from the Git website.
- **Windows:** Download the installer from the official Git website (https://git-scm.com/downloads). The installer will guide you through setup and provide access to the Git Bash command-line tool.
- **Linux:** Use your distribution's package manager. For example, on Debian/Ubuntu systems, use `sudo apt-get install git`.

Initial Configuration

After installation, open your terminal or command prompt and run these commands to set your global username and email for Git commits:

```
git config --global user.name "Your Name"
git config --global user.email
"your_email@example.com"
```

Step 2: Embracing the GitHub Community

1. **Head over to GitHub:** Visit the GitHub website (https://github.com/).
2. **Create your account:** Click "Sign up" and follow the on-screen prompts to create a free GitHub account. Choose a memorable username!
3. **Profile Power (optional):** Take some time to personalize your profile with a photo and a brief bio. It helps put a face to the code you'll be sharing.

Step 3: Starting Your Git-Managed Project

Let's initialize a Git repository for an existing project. Imagine you already have a folder containing your project files. Here's how to turn it into a Git repository:

1. **Navigate to your Project:** Open your terminal (or Git Bash on Windows) and use the cd command to navigate into your project directory. For instance:

```
cd /path/to/your/project
```

2. **Git Initiation:** Execute the following command:

```
git init
```

You'll see a message confirming that a hidden .git folder has been created within your project directory. This is where the magic of Git's version tracking resides!

Note: To create a **new** project and a Git repository simultaneously, simply create a new folder and then follow the steps above within that newly created folder.

Congratulations! Your Journey Begins

You're now on your way! You have Git installed, a GitHub account ready to connect with the world, and your first project under Git's protection. However, we're not done just yet.

The Magic of a Remote Repository (Optional)

While Git functions perfectly as a local version control tool, its true collaboration power shines when you connect with a remote repository on a platform like GitHub. Let's cover how to set that up in the next chapter, "Crafting Your Digital Space: Initiating a GitHub Repository."

Additional Resources

- **Git Downloads:** https://git-scm.com/downloads
- **Git Configuration:** https://git-scm.com/book/en/v2/Getting-Started-First-Time-Git-Setup
- **Creating a GitHub Account:** https://docs.github.com/en/get-started/signing-up-for-github

Get Ready to Dive Deeper

In the coming chapters, we'll explore how to use Git commands to take snapshots of your code, track changes, and collaborate like a pro. Onward!

Crafting Your Digital Space: Initiating a GitHub Repository

In the previous chapter, we set up Git locally and brought your project under its watchful eye. Now, it's time to extend your Git project's reach to the cloud by creating a remote home for it on GitHub.

Why a Remote Repository?

- **Backup & Safety:** Remote repositories act as an offsite backup, shielding your project from accidental deletion or hardware failures on your local machine.
- **Collaboration Central:** GitHub is built for collaboration. It lets you easily share your code, invite others to contribute, and manage changes from multiple developers seamlessly.
- **Showcase:** GitHub acts as a portfolio, demonstrating your coding skills to potential collaborators and employers.
- **Open-Source Powerhouse:** GitHub is home to countless open-source projects, providing inspiration, fostering a sense of community, and allowing you to contribute to the broader development world.

Steps to Create a GitHub Repository

1. **Log in to GitHub:** Visit https://github.com/ and log in to your GitHub account.
2. **"New Repository" Button:** On your GitHub dashboard, locate the "+" icon in the top-right corner and click it. Select "New repository."
3. **Repository Setup:**
   - **Repository name:** Choose a short and descriptive name for your project (e.g., "my-awesome-website").
   - **Description:** Add a brief explanation of your project's purpose (optional but recommended).
   - **Public / Private:** Decide whether you want your repository to be visible to the world (public) or accessible only to you and selected collaborators (private).
   - **Initialize with a README:** Tick this checkbox to automatically create a basic README file in your repository.

- ○ **Add .gitignore:** Consider selecting a suitable .gitignore template based on the programming languages and frameworks you're using (this helps prevent untracked files from cluttering your repo).
- ○ **Choose a license:** If you're open to others using and modifying your code, choose an open-source license (this defines how others can interact with your project).
4. **Click "Create repository":** Ta-da! Your GitHub repository is born.

Connecting Your Local and Remote Repositories

Now, let's link your local Git repository with this newly created remote repository on GitHub:

1. **Copy Remote Repository URL:** On your GitHub repository page, find the "Code" button. Click it, and get the repository's URL (it should look something like `https://github.com/your-username/my-awesome-website.git`).
2. **Remote Connection (in your terminal):** Navigate to your local project directory in your terminal and execute the following command, replacing the placeholder with your actual repository URL:

```
git remote add origin
https://github.com/your-username/my-awesome-website.git
```

   The term "origin" is a common alias used for the main remote repository.

3. **Time to Push!** Let's send your local Git history to GitHub with the following command:

```
git push -u origin main
```

   This command pushes your commits from your local 'main' (or 'master') branch to the 'main' branch of your remote repository on GitHub.

Success! Refresh your GitHub repository page; your code should now be safely stored and visible on GitHub.

Additional Tips

- **README Brilliance:** Your README file is the first thing people see when they visit your repository. Use it to provide a clear project description, setup instructions, and contribution guidelines.
- **Commits Before Pushing:** It's best practice to make some initial commits to your local repository before your first push to GitHub. This way, you're not sending an empty project.

The Collaboration Doorway

With your project now residing on GitHub, you've unlocked a world of collaborative possibilities. You can invite others, work on features together, and contribute to existing open-source projects.

Additional Resources

- **Creating a Repository on GitHub:** https://docs.github.com/en/repositories/creating-and-managing-repositories/creating-a-new-repository
- **Git Remote Documentation:** https://git-scm.com/docs/git-remote

Command Line Chronicles: Mastering the Git Command Line Interface

While there are various graphical tools (GUIs) for Git, the command line remains the most powerful and versatile way to interact with your repositories. Think of it as gaining access to the full range of Git's superpowers.

Why the Command Line?

- **Speed & Efficiency:** For many actions, the command line is simply faster than clicking through menus in a GUI.
- **Automation:** Command line tools can be scripted and integrated into your development workflows for automation.
- **Universality:** Command line knowledge translates seamlessly across operating systems (Windows, macOS, Linux).
- **Unlocking Hidden Features:** Some Git features are primarily or only accessible through the command line.

Embracing the Terminal

If you're new to the command line, don't panic! Here's a quick primer:

- **Terminals & Shells:** Common terminals include "Terminal" (macOS), "Git Bash" (Windows), or the default terminal on most Linux systems. The shell is the command interpreter within the terminal (e.g., Bash, Zsh).
- **Navigation:** Get comfortable with these basics:
    - `ls` (or `dir` on Windows): List directory contents
    - `cd directory_name`: Change into a directory
    - `cd ..`: Move up one level in the directory structure
    - `pwd`: Shows your current location

Important Notes:

- **Case Sensitivity:** Commands and filenames in the terminal are usually case-sensitive!

- **Git is Always Watching:** Git needs to know the context, i.e., you must be within a Git repository directory for most Git commands to work.

Essential Git Commands

Let's explore some of the core commands you'll frequently use on your Git adventures:

1. **Initialization**
   - `git init:` Transforms the current directory into a Git repository. Remember, we've used this in a previous chapter!
2. **Cloning a Remote Repository**
- `git clone repository_url:` Downloads a copy of an existing remote repository to your local machine, creating a complete Git project.
3. **Staging and Committing**
   - `git status:` Summarizes the state of your project, showing changed files, untracked files, and the current branch. Your best friend!
   - `git add file_name:` Adds a specific file to the staging area.
   - `git add .` Stages all modified and new files.
   - `git commit -m "Clear commit message":` Captures the staged changes with a descriptive message.
4. **History Navigation**
   - `git log:` Displays a chronological log of past commits with details like commit ID, author, date, and message.
5. **Synchronizing with Remotes**
- `git push origin main:` Sends your committed changes from your local 'main' branch to the 'main' branch of the remote repository named 'origin' (GitHub, for example).
- `git pull origin main:` Fetches changes from the remote 'main' branch and merges them into your local 'main' branch.

Additional Power Commands (a glimpse)

- `git branch:` Lists branches, creates new branches.

- `git checkout branch_name:` Switches to a different branch.
- `git merge branch_name:` Merges changes from another branch.

Practice Makes Perfect

The best way to master Git commands is to use them! Create practice repositories, experiment, and don't be afraid to try things out. If you get stuck, `git help` is your lifeline, providing information about any Git command.

Additional Resources

- **Interactive Git Cheatsheet:** https://training.github.com/downloads/github-git-cheat-sheet/
- **Try Git Online Tutorial:** https://try.github.io/
- **Git Documentation:** https://git-scm.com/docs

Pro Tip: Create aliases for frequently used Git commands to save typing and speed up your workflow (This is a tad more advanced, but worth exploring later!)

Next Up: Setting Up Your Environment

A well-configured development environment makes your Git journey smoother. In the next chapter, we'll cover installation guides and customization tips!

Git Installation Guide: Setting Up Your Developer Environment

Before wielding the power of Git, it's essential to have it correctly installed and configured on your development machine. While the overall process is simple, there are some nuances depending on your operating system. Let's break it down.

Step 1: Check for an Existing Installation

Sometimes, Git might already be lurking on your system, let's verify:

1. **Open your terminal:** This might be 'Terminal' on macOS, 'Git Bash' on Windows, or your default Linux terminal.
2. **Test Command:** Type `git --version` and press Enter. If Git is installed, it will report its version number.

Step 2: Installation (if needed)

If Git is absent, let's get it set up:

- **macOS**
1. **Xcode Command Line Tools (Recommended):** The easiest way is to install Xcode Command Line Tools. Type the following in your terminal, which will trigger the installation process:

```
xcode-select --install
```

2. **Alternative: Git Installer:** Download the official installer from the Git website (https://git-scm.com/downloads).
- **Windows**
  - **Git for Windows Installer:** Download the installer directly from the Git website (https://git-scm.com/downloads). Follow the on-screen installation instructions. This conveniently includes Git Bash, a Git-friendly command-line environment.
- **Linux**
  - **Debian/Ubuntu systems:** Use your package manager:

```
sudo apt-get update
```

```
sudo apt-get install git
```

- ○ **Other Linux distributions:** Consult your distribution's documentation for the specific package manager command (e.g., yum for Fedora-based distributions).

Step 3: Basic Configuration (For Everyone)

With Git installed, let's fine-tune your initial setup:

1. **Set your identity:** Tell Git who you are – this information gets added to your commits. Execute these commands in your terminal:

```
git config --global user.name "Your Name"
git config --global user.email
"your_email@example.com"
```

2. **Optional – Default Text Editor:** Git might need a text editor for certain operations. You can set your preferred editor (e.g., Vim, Nano):

```
git config --global core.editor nano
```

Replace 'nano' with the command to open your chosen editor.

Step 4: Choose and Customize Your Text Editor / IDE

A good text editor or Integrated Development Environment (IDE) significantly enhances your Git experience. Here's the gist, but explore and choose what suits you best:

- **Popular Text Editors:**
  - ○ Sublime Text: https://www.sublimetext.com/
  - ○ Atom: https://atom.io/
  - ○ VS Code: https://code.visualstudio.com/ (Amazing Git integration)
- **IDEs:**
  - ○ IntelliJ IDEA: https://www.jetbrains.com/idea/
  - ○ WebStorm: https://www.jetbrains.com/webstorm/
  - ○ PyCharm: https://www.jetbrains.com/pycharm/

Git Integration: Many text editors and IDEs have built-in Git support or extensions/plugins, providing visual tools to manage your repositories.

Step 5: Enhancing Your Terminal (Optional)

- **Colors and Aesthetics:** Customizing your terminal with color-coding and visual enhancements can make using Git more pleasant and efficient. Tools like 'Oh My Zsh' (https://ohmyz.sh/) are popular for this.

Additional Resources

- **Git's Official Setup Guide:** https://git-scm.com/book/en/v2/Getting-Started-Installing-Git
- **Choosing a Text Editor:** Many comparison resources and discussions exist online to help you decide.

Verification

Double-check that everything works by creating a test repository. Open your terminal, navigate to a suitable directory, and execute:

```
git init
```

Success? Time to start managing your code like a pro!

Next Up: Creating Repositories

Now that your environment is ready, we'll dive into creating Git repositories to safeguard your projects effectively.

Local Repository Creation - Part One

In the previous chapters, we unraveled the power of Git and GitHub as essential tools for managing your coding projects. We established a solid understanding of the core concepts that underpin these platforms. With this foundation laid, we are now ready to embark on a practical adventure—the creation of your first local Git repository.

Think of your local repository as your project's personal command center on your computer. It's a hidden haven where Git meticulously tracks every modification and snapshot of your code, creating a historical timeline of your development journey.

In this chapter, we'll dive into the process of setting up a local repository, initializing it with Git, and understanding the fundamental structure that powers this system. By the end of this journey, you'll have a robust local foundation ready to store and manage your project files.

Understanding Local Repositories: The Heart of Version Control

Let's dissect the core purpose of local repositories within the Git ecosystem:

- **Offline Development:** Local repositories grant you the freedom to work on your projects independently, without requiring a constant internet connection. This fosters a more focused and streamlined coding experience.
- **Granular Version Tracking:** Every change you make—from adding lines of code to deleting files—is meticulously recorded within your local repository, providing a comprehensive history of your project's evolution.
- **Safe Experimentation:** Local repositories encourage experimentation by serving as a playground where you can test new features or refactor code without the risk of disrupting a shared project workspace.
- **Foundation for Collaboration:** Your local repository acts as the base from which you can share your work with others on platforms like GitHub, driving efficient teamwork.

The Initialization Dance: Creating Your Local Repository

Let's break down the steps involved in bringing a local repository to life:

1. **Project Home:** Start by deciding where you want to store your project on your computer. Create a new folder to act as its dedicated home.
2. **Git Initiation Command:** Open a command-line interface (like your Terminal on Mac or Linux or Git Bash on Windows) and navigate to this newly created project folder. Next, let's perform the initialization magic with the following command:

   ```
   git init
   ```

   This command tells Git, "Hey, I'd like to establish a new version control kingdom right here in this folder!"

Hidden Haven of Git: Upon running `git init`, a hidden `.git` subdirectory appears inside your project folder. This is the nerve center of your local repository, meticulously storing all the historical records and version control data that Git needs to work its magic. It's essential to avoid tampering with this folder, as it contains the heart of your project's history.

Exploring the .git Subdirectory: What Lies Beneath

While hidden, the `.git` subdirectory houses an intricate structure that powers Git's tracking capabilities. Let's briefly examine some of its key components:

- **objects:** This is where Git stores the actual snapshots of your code, file modifications, and other versioned data as compressed objects. Think of this as Git's long-term memory bank.
- **refs:** The `refs` folder contains pointers to different points in your project's history, such as branches and commits. This allows Git to navigate back and forth along your development timeline.
- **HEAD:** This is a special file that tells Git what your currently active branch is. It's like your "you are here" marker within your project's version history.

Additional Resources:

- **Git Documentation - git init:** https://git-scm.com/docs/git-init
- **Git for Beginners (video):**
  https://www.youtube.com/watch?v=hwP7WQkmECE

Coming Up Next...

With your local repository established, you have a solid foundation on which to build your project. In the next chapter (Local Repository Creation - Part Two), we'll delve into adding your first files to Git's watchful eye and learn the art of staging your changes.

Local Repository Creation - Part Two

Welcome back! In the previous chapter, we laid the groundwork for your project's evolution by establishing a local Git repository. Now, let's breathe life into this repository by learning how to add your project's files to Git's watchful eye. We'll delve into the staging area, a crucial stepping stone in the process of crafting well-organized commits.

Introducing Files: Populating Your Repository

Let's imagine your project consists of the following files:

- `index.html`
- `main.css`
- `script.js`

Currently, these files reside within your project folder, but they are completely oblivious to the existence of your Git repository. Let's change that!

1. The "git status" Command: Your Repository's Pulse

Before we start adding files willy-nilly, let's use a handy command to get a snapshot of the situation:

```
git status
```

This command provides valuable insights. You'll likely see a message along the lines of "Untracked files," followed by a list of your project files. Git is telling you, "Hey, I see these files, but I'm not actively tracking any changes to them yet."

2. "git add": The Gateway to Tracking

To start tracking changes to a file, we'll use the `git add` command. Here are a couple of ways you can use it:

- **Adding a Single File:** For example, to add `index.html`:

  ```
  git add index.html
  ```

- **Adding Multiple Files:** To add both `main.css` and `script.js`:

  ```
  git add main.css script.js
  ```

- **Adding Everything at Once (Use with Caution):** To add all files in your current project folder, use a period:

  ```
  git add .
  ```

  Caution: Use the `git add .` command carefully! It will add everything, even potentially unnecessary temporary files.

Detour: The Staging Area – The "Almost Committed" Zone

Behind the scenes, the `git add` command places the files you add into a special holding area known as the staging area (or index). The staging area is like a workbench where you carefully select and prepare changes that you intend to bundle together as a single commit.

Why do we need this staging area? Here are a few reasons:

- **Granular Control:** It gives you fine-grained control over what goes into a commit, preventing accidental inclusion of unrelated file changes.
- **Focused Development:** The staging area helps you break down large changes into smaller, more logical, and easy-to-review commits.
- **Polished Commits:** Before committing, you can ensure that only relevant changes are included, allowing you to craft clean and meaningful snapshots of your project's history.

3. Verify with "git status"

- Execute `git status` once again. You'll notice the output has changed. Files staged with `git add` will now be listed in green under "Changes to be committed," meaning they're ready and waiting to be sealed into your repository's history!

Additional Resources:

- **Git Documentation - git add:** https://git-scm.com/docs/git-add
- **Understanding Git Staging Area (Article):**
  https://www.atlassian.com/git/tutorials/saving-changes/git-add

Coming Up Next…

With files staged, you're ready to take the next step: Committing your work! In the next chapter, we'll dive into the art of committing and master the techniques essential for preserving your project's evolution.

Section 2:
Core Concepts Demystified

Committing to Excellence: Understanding the Art of Commits

In the previous chapters, we initialized your local repository and learned how to add files to the staging area, placing them in a "ready-to-go" state. Now, it's time to seal those changes into your project's history with the powerful "commit" command.

Think of a Git commit as a snapshot of your project at a specific point in time. Every commit captures the state of your codebase, along with any associated changes. This allows you to revisit past versions, explore different development paths, and even roll back undesired modifications.

In this chapter, we'll dissect the commit process, explore best practices for writing meaningful commit messages, and reveal how commits form an invisible timeline within your repository.

The Essence of "git commit"

Let's break down the key steps involved in creating a commit:

1. **Staging Your Changes:** Ensure that all the necessary files and modifications you intend to include in the commit are present in the staging area using the `git add` command.
2. **Crafting Your Commit Message:** At the heart of every commit lies the commit message. Use the `git commit` command with the -m flag to provide a short yet descriptive message:

```
git commit -m "Add initial HTML, CSS, and JavaScript files"
```

3. **A New Link in the Chain** Upon execution of `git commit`, Git takes a snapshot of the staged files, records the commit message, and forges a new link in your repository's historical chain. Each commit receives a unique identification hash (a long string of letters and numbers) acting as its fingerprint in the repository.

Commit Best Practices: Messages that Matter

A well-written commit message is invaluable for understanding your project's development process. Here are some tips for crafting clear and informative commit messages:

- **Keep it Concise:** The first line should be a brief summary (think 50 characters or less) that quickly communicates the overall change made in the commit.
- **Present Tense:** Write your commit messages in the present tense. For example, "Add signup functionality" instead of "Added signup functionality."
- **Provide Context** If necessary, use the following lines to expand on the commit, giving more details about the rationale behind the changes.
- **Reference Issues (Optional):** If your commit addresses or resolves specific issues in an issue tracker, include their IDs in the message (e.g., "Fixes #42").

Unraveling the Commit Timeline with "git log"

With every commit, Git diligently tracks your project's evolution. Let's use the `git log` command to explore this historical record:

```
git log
```

Each commit will be displayed, accompanied by its unique hash, author, date, and the commit message. This is your project's "time travel" log, allowing you to revisit past states as needed.

Pro Tip: The `git log` command has various options to customize how your commit history is displayed. Experiment with flags like `--oneline` for a condensed summary or `--graph` to visualize the branching structure of your repository.

Additional Resources

- **Git Documentation - git commit:**
  https://git-scm.com/docs/git-commit
- **Good Commit Messages Guide:**
  https://chris.beams.io/posts/git-commit/
- **Git Log Formatting:**
  https://git-scm.com/book/en/v2/Git-Basics-Viewing-the-Commit-History

Coming Up Next...

Now that you have a solid grasp of commits, it's time to delve deeper, exploring more granular control over commits and techniques for modifying your project's history.

Stay tuned, as the journey continues!

Commit Mastery: Digging Deeper into the Commit Process

In the previous chapter, we grasped the fundamentals of making commits using the `git commit` command and learned how to write informative commit messages. Now it's time to expand your Git toolbox with techniques that give you even more control over how your changes are incorporated.

Amending Your Last Commit

Occasionally, you may realize that you missed a small change, made a typo in your commit message, or simply want to add another file right after committing. Enter the `--amend` flag:

1. **Staging Additional Changes:** If necessary, add any forgotten files using `git add`.
2. **Modifying the Message:** Execute the following command:

   ```
   git commit --amend -m "Updated commit message"
   ```

   This opens your text editor to modify the previous commit message.

Caution: The `--amend` option effectively rewrites the most recent commit. Avoid using it on commits already pushed to a shared remote repository, as it can cause conflicts and confusion for others working on the project.

The "Unstaging" Dance: Removing Files from a Commit

Imagine you've staged a file using `git add` but later change your mind. How do you remove it from the staging area? Here's where `git restore` comes to the rescue:

- **Unstaging a Specific File:**

  ```
  git restore --staged <file_name>
  ```

- **Unstaging All Staged Files:** Be cautious, as this will unstage everything:

```
git restore --staged .
```

Splitting Commits: Granularity is Key

Sometimes, you might find yourself working on multiple features or changes and inadvertently stage them all together. To create smaller, more focused commits, let's learn how to split them apart:

1. **Interactive Rebase with "git rebase -i":** Use `git log` to identify the commit (using its hash) BEFORE where you want to perform the split. Then, type:

   ```
   git rebase -i <commit_hash>
   ```

   This opens an editor listing commits. Replace 'pick' with 'edit' next to the commit you want to split. Save and exit.

2. **Resetting to the Target Commit:**

   ```
   git reset --soft HEAD^
   ```

   (This undoes the commit, but leaves your changes staged)

3. **Divide and Conquer:** Unstage some files (`git restore --staged`), create a new commit (`git commit`), restage the remaining files, and create another commit.

Note: Interactive rebasing involves rewriting a project's history and should generally be avoided on shared branches. Use with caution!

Additional Resources

- **Git Documentation - git commit amend:**
  https://git-scm.com/docs/git-commit#Documentation/git-commit.txt---amend

- **Git Documentation - git restore:**
  https://git-scm.com/docs/git-restore
- **Git Documentation - git rebase:**
  https://git-scm.com/docs/git-rebase

Coming Up Next…

With these advanced commit manipulation techniques, you're well on your way to achieving cleaner, more organized project histories. In the next chapter, we'll explore the staging area in greater detail, providing additional strategies for managing your code changes prior to committing.

Staging Grounds: Preparing Your Code for Deployment

In previous chapters, we've learned that the staging area (or "index") is a temporary holding space for changes. It allows you to finely control which modified files and edits are included in your next commit. Think of it as the workbench where you assemble your project's evolution, one piece at a time.

In this chapter, we'll uncover more advanced staging techniques, learn how to inspect what's in the staging area, and understand how its use contributes to polished and meaningful commits.

Selective Staging: Focusing Your Commits

Sometimes, you may have worked on numerous files and only want to include a subset of changes in a single commit. Here's where some staging finesse comes in handy:

- **Staging Individual Files:** You've seen this in earlier chapters—use `git add file1 file2 ...` to add selected files.
- **Staging Parts of a File (Hunk Staging):** Git lets you stage smaller sections within a modified file!
    1. **Interactive Addition:** Execute `git add -p <file_name>`. Git will present you with 'hunks' (chunks of changes) within the file.
    2. **Choose:** Type 'y' to stage a hunk, 'n' to skip it, 's' to split a hunk further, and more!

"git status": Your Staging Area Compass

The `git status` command remains your invaluable guide. It provides a clear breakdown of your project's state:

- **Files Not Staged:** Changes that are not yet included in your next commit.
- **Files Staged:** Changes ready and waiting to be committed.

Visualizing Differences

To understand the exact changes that have been made, let's utilize these helpful commands:

- **"git diff"**: Without any additional arguments, `git diff` shows you unstaged changes. Perfect for a final review before adding files.
- **"git diff –staged"**: Focuses exclusively on staged changes. This gives you a last glance to verify what will be included in your commit.

Unstaging: A Step Backwards

We've covered how to remove files completely from the staging area using `git restore --staged`. But what if you only want to unstage selective parts within a file? Here's how:

1. **Start Interactive Unstaging:** Use `git restore --staged -p <file_name>`. This works similarly to interactive staging, presenting hunks within the file.
2. **Undo Staging:** Type 'n' to unstage a hunk that you've already added.

Resetting Individual Files

Imagine you staged a file then made more changes you *don't* want included in the commit:

`git restore --staged <file_name>` resets the file in the staging area back to the version of the last commit, while keeping further modifications in your working directory.

Important Note: `git restore --staged` should not be confused with `git reset`. They serve different purposes. `restore` is primarily for manipulating the staging area, while `reset` can modify your project history.

Additional Resources

- **Git Documentation - git diff:** [https://git-scm.com/docs/git-diff] (https://git-scm.com/docs/git-diff)
- **Hunk Staging Explained:** https://git-scm.com/book/en/v2/Git-Tools-Interactive-Staging

Coming Up Next…

With an enhanced understanding of the staging area, you now have the ability to craft precisely tailored commits. Up next, we'll embark on a journey into the world of branches – where parallel lines of development converge and diverge!

Branching Out: Exploring Git Branches - Part One

Until now, we've primarily visualized your Git repository as a linear path of commits. Branches introduce a powerful new dimension, allowing your project's history to diverge into multiple timelines. You can work on different features or experiments independently without disrupting the main flow of your project.

The Essence of Branches

At its core, a Git branch is simply a lightweight pointer to a specific commit within your repository. Here's the key takeaway: **When you create a new branch, Git doesn't copy your entire project. It simply creates a new pointer!** This makes branches fast and efficient.

Let's illustrate:

1. **The "main" Branch:** By default, Git starts you off with a branch traditionally named `main` (or sometimes `master`). This is your project's primary development line.
2. **Branching Off:** As you work, you might decide to create a new branch called `new-feature` to experiment with a new idea. Initially, this branch points to the same commit as your `main` branch.
3. **Divergence:** You add commits on the `new-feature` branch, and its pointer moves forward, independent of the `main` branch.

Why Branches Matter

Let's examine some compelling reasons why branches are a vital part of the Git workflow:

- **Focused Development:** A dedicated branch provides a focused workspace for implementing a specific feature or bug fix.
- **Safe Experimentation:** Branches let you test potentially disruptive changes without impacting the stability of your `main` branch. If the experiment fails, simply delete the branch!

- **Collaboration:** Working on separate branches facilitates teamwork. Each developer can work in their own sandbox, making it easier to integrate everyone's changes later.

Basic Branch Management

Let's get hands-on with some essential branch-related commands:

- **Creating a Branch:** To create a new branch:

```
git branch <branch_name>
```

- **Listing Branches:** Check out all existing branches:

```
git branch
```

  The branch you're currently on will be marked with an asterisk.

- **Switching Branches:** Hop between branches effortlessly:

```
git checkout <branch_name>
```

"git checkout": Master of Disguise

The `git checkout` command has a dual purpose:

1. **Switching Branches:** As demonstrated above.
2. **Creating AND Switching:** A time-saving shortcut is combining branch creation with switching:

```
git checkout -b <new_branch>
```

Additional Resources

- **Git Branching Basics:** https://git-scm.com/book/en/v2/Git-Branching-Basic-Branching-and-Merging
- **Interactive Branching Tutorial:** https://learngitbranching.js.org/

Coming Up Next…

In the next chapter, we'll continue our branching journey by learning how to merge branches, inspect differences between branches, and visualize your project's branching structure.

Branching Out: Exploring Git Branches - Part Two

In the previous chapter, we learned about the fundamentals of branches, how to create them, and how to switch between them. Now, let's explore the process of bringing the work done on separate branches together and maintaining a clean system of branches as your project evolves.

Merging: Uniting the Branches

When you're satisfied with the changes on a branch, it's time to integrate them into your main development line. That's where the `git merge` command enters the picture:

1. **Check Your Location:** Start by switching to the branch you want to merge into (often your `main` branch):

   ```
   git checkout main
   ```

2. **The Merge Dance:** Execute the following command to bring in the changes from another branch:

   ```
   git merge <branch_to_merge>
   ```

Types of Merges

Git offers two primary ways to perform a merge:

- **Fast-Forward Merge:** If your branch progresses in a strictly linear fashion from the target branch, Git can perform a "fast-forward" merge. It simply advances the target branch's pointer forward to the latest commit of the branch being merged.
- **Three-Way Merge:** When branches have diverged, Git creates a new "merge commit" that attempts to reconcile the differences from both branches, uniting the changes. If conflicts arise that Git cannot resolve automatically, you'll be prompted to address them manually.

Inspecting Differences Before Merging

Before merging, it's wise to preview changes. Use `git diff` between the branches:

```
git diff <current_branch> <branch_to_merge>
```

Visualizing with "git log –graph"

To get a broader picture of your project's history and branching structure, try this:

```
git log --graph --decorate --oneline
```

This adds visual cues, showing how branches connect and diverge.

Deleting Branches: Keeping Things Neat

Once a branch has been merged, you might want to clean up. **Caution:** Only delete branches you're sure you don't need anymore. Here's how:

```
git branch -d <branch_to_delete>
```

Git will prevent you from deleting the branch you're currently on. To force deletion (use with care!), use a capital '-D'.

Important Note: Deleting a branch in your local repository does not automatically delete its counterpart on a remote repository (like on GitHub).

Additional Resources

- **Git Documentation - git merge:**
  https://git-scm.com/docs/git-merge
- **Understanding Git Merge Conflicts:**
  https://www.atlassian.com/git/tutorials/using-branches/merge-conflicts

Coming Up Next…

With the ability to create, switch, merge, and delete branches, you now have powerful tools for managing multiple lines of development. Next, we'll explore how to use `git status` and delve into ways to inspect specific commits, providing insights into your project's evolution.

Status Checks and Commit Inspection: Understanding Your Code's Pulse

We've learned how Git diligently tracks every modification made to your project. But how do you effectively interpret this wealth of historical data? In this chapter, we'll master the tools Git provides to stay informed about your repository's status, examine individual commits, and even compare different versions of your code.

Your Constant Companion: "git status"

The `git status` command is your lifeline for understanding the current state of your repository. Let's recap its key functions:

- **Untracked Files:** Are there new files Git hasn't started tracking yet?
- **Changes to Tracked Files:** Have existing files been modified, and are they staged or unstaged?
- **Branches:** Which branch are you currently working on?
- **Staying Ahead/Behind:** Are there commits on your local branch or its remote counterpart that need syncing?

Inspecting Individual Commits

The `git log` command introduced earlier provides a basic overview of your project history. Now, let's dig deeper.

- **Examining Commit Details with "git show":** To reveal the changes introduced in a specific commit, use:

  ```
  git show <commit_hash>
  ```

  This displays the commit message, author, date, and a detailed list of changes (the diff).

Comparing Commits with "git diff"

To understand what changed between two specific commits, this variation of `git diff` is essential:

```
git diff <commit_hash_1> <commit_hash_2>
```

This allows you to analyze the differences introduced across a range of commits.

Time Travel with "git checkout" (Revisited)

Recall that `git checkout` is mostly known for switching branches. It also has a hidden time-traveling talent:

- **Checking out Older Commits:** To temporarily explore an older snapshot of your project, use:

```
git checkout <commit_hash>
```

  Important: This puts you in a "detached HEAD" state. To return to your latest work, remember to switch back to a branch (`git checkout <branch_name>`).

Additional Resources

- **Git Documentation - git status:**
  https://git-scm.com/docs/git-status
- **Git Documentation - git log:** https://git-scm.com/docs/git-log
- **Git Documentation - git show:** https://git-scm.com/docs/git-show
- **Git Documentation - git diff:** https://git-scm.com/docs/git-diff

Coming Up Next…

With these investigative techniques, you're well-equipped to monitor your repository and dissect the changes made within it. Next up, we'll tackle 'push' and 'pull,' the commands at the heart of syncing your local Git repository with remote counterparts like GitHub.

Push and Pull Dynamics: Synchronizing Your Repositories - Part One

Up until now, your Git journey has predominantly been a local affair. In this chapter, we'll venture into the realm of remote repositories, learning how to share your code with others and mirror your project onto platforms like GitHub. This is where collaboration begins to unfold!

Understanding Remote Repositories

Think of a remote repository as a copy of your project hosted on a centralized server accessible via the internet. Platforms like GitHub, GitLab, and Bitbucket provide the space to host these remote repositories:

- **Storage and Backup:** Remote repositories offer a safe haven for your project off your local machine, shielding your work from accidental loss.
- **Collaboration Hub:** Remote repositories act as a centralized meeting point, allowing teams or individuals to share and contribute to the same project.
- **Open Source Glory:** Platforms like GitHub offer a vibrant community where you can showcase your projects and even contribute to others' work.

Linking Your Local and Remote Repositories with "git remote"

Let's dissect the command that establishes the connection between your local repository and its remote counterpart:

- **Adding a Remote:**

```
git remote add <short_name> <repository_url>
```

  Popular short names include 'origin' for the main remote repository. The URL is provided by the remote hosting platform (like GitHub).

- **Listing Remotes:** To verify your remote links, use:

```
git remote -v
```

Pushing: Sending Your Commits Upstream

The `git push` command lets you upload your local commits to a remote repository, making them visible to others:

```
git push <remote_short_name> <branch_name>
```

For example, to push your local 'main' branch to the remote named 'origin':

```
git push origin main
```

Behind or Ahead?

You'll often see the output of `git push` indicating whether your local branch is "ahead" or "behind" the remote. This means:

- **Ahead:** Your local branch contains commits that haven't yet been pushed to the remote.
- **Behind:** The remote branch has commits that haven't made it into your local repository.

Pulling: Fetching Updates From a Remote

Just as `git push` uploads, `git pull` is the command to download updates from the remote repository, integrating them into your local branch:

```
git pull <remote_short_name> <branch_name>
```

A Note on Best Practices

It's a good habit to perform `git pull` to grab the latest changes from the remote repository *before* you start working on new features. This helps minimize potential conflicts later when integrating your work with others.

Additional Resources

- **Git Documentation - git remote:**
  https://git-scm.com/docs/git-remote
- **Git Documentation - git push:** https://git-scm.com/docs/git-push
- **Git Documentation - git pull:** https://git-scm.com/docs/git-pull

Coming Up Next...

We've covered the essentials of pushing changes to and fetching them from remote repositories. In the next chapter, we'll delve into typical push and pull workflows and strategies for gracefully handling conflicts when they arise.

Push and Pull Dynamics: Synchronizing Your Repositories - Part Two

In the previous chapter, we laid the foundation for interacting with remote repositories. Now, let's put the concepts of push and pull into practice, learning how to gracefully integrate work from remote branches and address potential conflicts.

The Fetch and Merge Workflow: A Safer Approach

While `git pull` can fetch and directly merge commits from a remote branch, there's a refined workflow offering greater control:

1. **Fetch Updates:** Start by fetching changes from the remote:

   ```
   git fetch <remote_short_name>
   ```

   This downloads the updates locally but doesn't automatically modify your working files.

2. **Examine Differences:** Carefully compare your local branch and the updated remote branch using `git diff`
3. **Merge (When Ready):** Once satisfied, merge the fetched commits into your local branch:

   ```
   git merge <remote_short_name>/<branch_name>
   ```

Understanding Conflicts

When concurrent changes are made to the same lines of code, a conflict may arise. Git will pause the merge process and highlight these conflicts in your files. Here's how to tackle it:

1. **Locate Conflicts:** Git marks conflict zones in your files with special markers (e.g., <«««, =======, »»»>).
2. **Manual Resolution:** Open the affected files. Choose between the changes from your local version or the incoming remote version. Delete the conflict markers and retain the desired code segments.
3. **Mark as Resolved:** Use `git add` to stage the resolved file(s).

4. **Finalize the Merge:** Complete the merge with:

```
git commit
```

Tips for Minimizing Conflicts

- **Commit and Push Frequently:** Smaller, focused commits make conflicts less likely and easier to resolve. Push often to stay in sync with the remote repository.
- **Pull Before Working:** Always fetch and merge the latest remote changes *before* starting new work on a branch.
- **Communicate with Your Team:** Coordinate with others working on the same project to reduce the likelihood of conflicting edits.

Rebase: An Alternative to Merging for Cleaner History

In certain cases, you might prefer a more linear project history. The `git rebase` command provides a way to 're-apply' your local commits on top of an updated remote branch. **Caution:** Rebasing rewrites history – use judiciously, especially in shared projects

Additional Resources

- **Understanding Git Conflicts:** https://www.atlassian.com/git/tutorials/using-branches/merge-conflicts
- **Git Documentation - git rebase:** https://git-scm.com/docs/git-rebase

Coming Up Next…

With these conflict resolution techniques, you can confidently synchronize repositories and tackle code divergence. Next, we'll explore how to undo or redo changes, a valuable skill to correct mistakes and experiment freely.

Reversing Time: Undoing and Redoing Changes - Part One

Git's powerful versioning system is your safety net, allowing you to experiment with confidence. In this chapter, we'll delve into techniques for undoing modifications, traveling back to earlier snapshots, and uncovering 'lost' commits. Consider this your time travel guide within the Git universe!

Scenario 1: Undoing Unstaged Changes

You've modified a file but realize the changes are incorrect. If the changes *aren't yet staged*, `git restore` comes to the rescue:

```
git restore <file_name>
```

This reverts the file back to its last committed version in your working directory. For all unstaged files, use a period: `git restore .`

Scenario 2: Modifying Your Last Commit

You've committed changes prematurely or made a mistake in your commit message. We introduced `git commit --amend` previously, which allows you to refine your last commit.

Scenario 3: Reverting to a Previous Commit with "git reset"

Let's say you want to roll back several commits, effectively undoing a chunk of your work. Enter the powerful `git reset`. There are different modes of reset:

- **`git reset --soft <commit_hash>`:** This resets your branch pointer to the specified commit but keeps your modifications both staged and unstaged in your working directory. This is useful if you want to restructure the history into different commits.
- **`git reset --mixed <commit_hash>`:** The default mode. It resets the branch pointer and unstages changes, but the changes remain in your working directory.

- **`git reset --hard <commit_hash>`: Proceed with Caution!** This forcefully resets everything. Both your branch pointer and working directory are modified to match the specified commit. Changes since then are discarded.

Important: `git reset --hard` can result in lost work. Use it judiciously!

A Word on Reflog: Retrieving 'Lost' Commits

Even if you accidentally remove commits, Git diligently tracks your actions in the reflog.

- **Listing History:**

```
git reflog
```

The reflog is your insurance policy. If you discover a commit you thought was 'lost' isn't lost at all, you can use the reflog to reset your branch back to that point.

Additional Resources

- **Git Documentation - git restore:** https://git-scm.com/docs/git-restore
- **Git Documentation - git reset:** https://git-scm.com/docs/git-reset
- **Git Documentation - git reflog:** https://git-scm.com/docs/git-reflog

Coming Up Next...

In the next chapter, we'll conclude our exploration of reversing time by unraveling how to selectively revert specific changes using 'git checkout' and 'git revert' – ideal for pinpointed fixes in your project's history.

Let's continue mastering the art of time travel within the Git realm!

Reversing Time: Undoing and Redoing Changes - Part Two

In the previous chapter, we discussed broad ways to roll back to past commits. Now, let's get granular, focusing on methods to undo specific changes or introduce carefully crafted counter-commits for fine-grained control.

Scenario 4: Reverting Changes from a Past Commit with "git checkout"

Perhaps you've introduced changes in a past commit that you wish to selectively undo. Here's how to isolate and restore a file to its state from a previous commit:

```
git checkout <commit_hash> -- <file_name>
```

This pulls the older version of the specified file from the designated commit and places it into your working directory.

Scenario 5: Creating a New "Undo" Commit with "git revert"

Let's say you want to entirely undo the changes introduced in a previous commit while creating a clear historical record. This is where `git revert` shines:

```
git revert <commit_hash>
```

Git will perform the following:

1. Analyze the changes made in the specified commit.
2. Create a *new* commit that introduces the exact opposite changes, effectively canceling out the original commit.

Why Revert Instead of Reset?

- **Preserves History:** `git revert` maintains your project's history by creating a new record of the change. `git reset` alters history as if the unwanted commit didn't happen.

- **Collaboration-Friendly:** `git revert` is less disruptive for teams if the commit has been shared, as it avoids forcibly rewriting the shared project history.

Additional Resources

- **Git Documentation - git checkout:**
  https://git-scm.com/docs/git-checkout
- **Git Documentation - git revert:**
  https://git-scm.com/docs/git-revert

Key Takeaways

Let's recap some important points about undoing changes within Git:

- **No Change is Permanent:** Git is incredibly forgiving. Between the staging area, reset options, and the reflog, there's almost always a way to recover a different state of your project.
- **Granularity is Key:** Choose the right tool for the job. Use `restore` for unstaged changes, `reset` for comprehensive rollbacks, `checkout` for targeted file reversions, and `revert` when a clear undoing record is desired.
- **Caution with History Rewriting:** Avoid using commands like `reset --hard` on shared branches in collaborative environments, as it can cause confusion and conflicts for others.

Coming Up Next...

With these time-bending techniques at your disposal, you can confidently explore changes and recover if needed. Next, we'll venture into the world of integrating different branches with seamless branch merging.

Branch Merging Made Simple: Integrating Your Codebase

Branches provide you with isolated workspaces, fostering experimentation and parallel development. But ultimately, you'll want to integrate these changes back into your central development line, typically your `main` branch. This is where branch merging shines!

Recall: Types of Merges

We covered this briefly earlier, but a refresher is essential:

- **Fast-Forward Merge:** If your branch's history is strictly linear, Git can simply move the branch pointer of your target branch 'forward' to the latest commit in the branch you're merging in.
- **Three-Way Merge:** When histories diverge, Git creates a new "merge commit" representing the union of changes from both branches. If it cannot resolve differences automatically, you'll be prompted to address conflicts.

The Basic Merge Workflow

Let's outline the steps for performing a standard merge:

1. **Place Yourself on the Target Branch:** Start by switching to the branch you want to merge into (often your `main` branch):

```
git checkout main
```

2. **Execute the Merge:** Now, initiate the merge process:

```
git merge <branch_to_merge>
```

3. **Conflict Resolution (if necessary):** If conflicts arise, address them within the affected files, stage changes with `git add`, and finalize the merge commit with `git commit`.

Visualizing Merges with "git log –graph"

Recall this incredibly useful command:

```
git log --graph --decorate --oneline
```

This visualization helps make sense of how your merge brought together different lines of development.

Strategies for Smooth Merging

To make the merge process frictionless:

- **Frequent Merging:** Consider merging smaller, completed features back into your main branch more frequently. This minimizes the potential for massive, overwhelming merge conflicts.
- **Pre-Merge 'Fetch and Rebase':** If you're collaborating, consider fetching and rebasing your feature branch on the latest `main` branch before merging. This ensures a cleaner, more linear merge history.

A Note on Feature Branches

Feature branches are temporary branches created for specific tasks. Once the feature is ready and merged, it's often good practice to delete the feature branch (`git branch -d <feature_branch>`). This keeps your repository organized and free of unneeded clutter

Additional Resources

- **Git Basics - Branching and Merging:** https://git-scm.com/book/en/v2/Git-Branching-Basic-Branching-and-Merging
- **Atlassian Git Tutorial - Merging vs. Rebasing:** https://www.atlassian.com/git/tutorials/merging-vs-rebasing

Coming Up Next…

With merging mastered, you can seamlessly combine work from various branches. Next, we'll venture into the collaborative world of GitHub, exploring pull requests and the code review process – essential tools for teamwork!

Gateway to Collaboration: Navigating Pull Requests and Code Reviews - Part One

Until now, our Git adventures have largely been a solo endeavor. Pull requests and code reviews fundamentally change this dynamic, enabling you to propose changes to projects, get feedback, and collaborate effectively with others, whether within a company or the broader open-source community.

What is a Pull Request (PR)?

Think of a pull request as a bridge between your work and a shared codebase. Here's the basic flow:

1. **Development on a Branch:** You create a branch, make your changes, and carefully craft your commits.
2. **Submitting a Pull Request:** Using GitHub's interface, you formally propose merging your branch into a target branch (often the `main` branch) of the project you want to contribute to.
3. **Discussion and Review:** The pull request becomes a forum for discussion, code review, and potential iterations based on feedback from maintainers or other contributors.
4. **Merging (or Not):** Maintainers decide if the proposed changes are suitable. If so, your pull request is merged, integrating your work into the shared codebase!

Essential Elements of a Great Pull Request

- **Clear Title and Description:** Explain the purpose and scope of the changes you're proposing.
- **Concise and Focused:** Smaller PRs addressing specific changes are easier to review and less likely to introduce conflicts
- **Tests:** If you've added features, include tests to ensure code quality and prevent unforeseen bugs.

The Code Review Process

At the heart of a pull request lies the code review, where maintainers or other developers scrutinize proposed changes. This process aims to:

- **Maintain Code Quality:** Ensure changes align with the project's overall code quality standards.
- **Catch Potential Errors:** Reviewers can uncover bugs and suggest improvements before the code is integrated into the main branch.
- **Knowledge Sharing and Mentorship:** Code reviews foster a learning culture and allow both experienced and less experienced developers to exchange knowledge.

Tips for Effective Code Reviews

Whether you're submitting your code for review or acting as the reviewer:

- **Be Respectful and Constructive:** Offer feedback in a way that focuses on code improvement rather than personal criticism.
- **Provide Context:** Explain the rationale behind your decisions when providing feedback or proposing changes.
- **Stay Focused:** Discuss the specifics of the code changes. Avoid side tangents.

Additional Resources

- **GitHub Guides - About Pull Requests:**
  https://docs.github.com/en/pull-requests/collaborating-with-pull-requests/proposing-changes-to-your-work-with-pull-requests/about-pull-requests
- **Best Practices for Code Reviews:**
  https://google.github.io/eng-practices/review/reviewer/

Coming Up Next...

In the next part, we'll dive deeper into the practical aspects of using pull requests on GitHub, explore advanced techniques, and address common challenges in the code review process.

Gateway to Collaboration: Navigating Pull Requests and Code Reviews - Part Two

In the previous chapter, we explored the fundamental concepts underlying pull requests and code reviews. Now, it's time to translate these concepts into action on platforms like GitHub and refine our collaborative development processes.

GitHub Pull Request Workflow in Practice

Let's walk through a typical workflow for contributing to a project on GitHub:

1. **Forking the Repository (if necessary):** If you don't have write permissions to the main project, start by forking (creating your own copy) of the repository on GitHub
2. **Clone Locally:** Clone your fork of the repository to your computer using `git clone`.
3. **Branching and Development:** Create a dedicated feature branch for your changes and develop locally, following Git best practices (`git add`, `git commit` with meaningful messages).
4. **Push to Remote:** Push your branch to your fork (`git push origin <your_branch>`).
5. **Creating the Pull Request:** On GitHub, navigate to your fork and initiate a pull request comparing your feature branch to the appropriate target branch in the main repository. Include a clear description and title.
6. **Review and Discussion:** Maintainers and collaborators review your code, suggest changes, and discuss within the pull request interface.
7. **Iterate (if needed):** Address feedback, make necessary changes, and push additional commits to your feature branch. These updates automatically appear in the pull request.

10. **Approval and Merge:** Once the maintainers are satisfied, your pull request is merged, and your contributions are integrated into the main codebase.

Advanced Tip: Draft Pull Requests

For works in progress seeking early feedback, consider marking a pull request as a 'draft'. This signals it's not ready for final merging but invites discussion and collaboration.

Dealing with Merge Conflicts

If changes on the target branch conflict with yours, GitHub will flag them. You'll need to resolve conflicts locally:

1. Pull the latest changes from the upstream repository into your local branch.
2. Address merge conflicts as we did previously.
3. Add the resolved files (`git add`) and create a new commit.
4. Push the updated branch to your fork. The conflicts should resolve within the pull request automatically if done correctly.

Continuous Improvement

- **Respond Promptly:** Timely responses to feedback keep the review process moving and show respect for the maintainers' time.
- **Embrace Feedback:** View code review as a learning opportunity to improve your skills.
- **Reciprocate:** Participate in reviewing others' pull requests. You'll sharpen your code analysis skills and contribute back to the project.

Additional Resources

- **GitHub Workflow Guide:**
  https://docs.github.com/en/get-started/quickstart/github-flow
- **Handling Merge Conflicts: A Visual Guide:**
  https://www.atlassian.com/git/tutorials/using-branches/merge-conflicts

Coming Up Next…

With a solid grasp of code reviews and pull requests, you're ready to collaborate effectively on projects of any scale. Up next, let's explore some of Git's lesser-known but incredibly useful commands to add to your arsenal!

Exploring Git's Toolkit: Lesser-Known Commands Unveiled - Part One

While tools like 'commit', 'checkout', 'push', and 'pull' form the backbone of your Git usage, there's an entire suite of commands designed to make your life easier. In this chapter, we'll uncover some of these powerful and often overlooked commands.

1. "git stash": Your Temporary Pocket

Imagine you're working on a feature, but an urgent issue arises that requires immediate attention. You don't want to commit unfinished changes, yet you need a clean working directory. Here's where 'stash' comes to the rescue:

- **Saving Changes:**

  ```
  git stash
  ```

  This temporarily shelves your uncommitted changes, giving you a clean working state.

- **Retrieving Changes:**

  ```
  git stash pop
  ```

  Restores your stashed changes back to your working directory.

Use Cases for "git stash"

- Switching tasks rapidly without committing half-finished work.
- Cleaning your workspace before running tests or updates.
- Storing changes temporarily when addressing urgent matters.

2. "git bisect": Bug Detective

Tracking down the commit that introduced a bug can be tedious. `git bisect` turns you into a detective, making the process systematic:

1. **Initiate the Search:**

   ```
   git bisect start
   ```

2. **Mark Good and Bad:** You'll need to tell Git a known 'good' commit and a known 'bad' commit (containing the bug). Use `git bisect good <commit_hash>` and `git bisect bad <commit_hash>`

3. **The Hunt:** Git will checkout a commit between your bad and good state. Test your code. Mark the commit as 'good' or 'bad' accordingly.

4. **Zeroing In:** Git iteratively checks out commits, narrowing down the search until it reveals the culprit commit.

3. "git reflog": Your Undo Safety Net

We've mentioned the reflog previously when reversing changes. Let's explore it directly. Think of it as your ultimate undo history:

```
git reflog
```

The reflog tracks practically every action that modifies your repository's HEAD. If you mistakenly reset to the wrong commit, the reflog provides the hashes needed to recover your lost work.

4. "git shortlog": Summarizing Commit History

For a concise overview of commits grouped by author, use the following:

```
git shortlog
```

This is especially helpful for open-source projects or teams to get a quick summary of who has been contributing and the high-level changes they've made.

Additional Resources

- **Git Stash Documentation:** https://git-scm.com/docs/git-stash
- **Git Bisect Documentation:** https://git-scm.com/docs/git-bisect
- **Git Reflog Documentation:** https://git-scm.com/docs/git-reflog

Coming Up Next...

In the next chapter, we'll continue our journey through Git's hidden gems, unlocking tools for surgical changes, exploring aliases, and custom setups to streamline your workflows.

Exploring Git's Toolkit: Lesser-Known Commands Unveiled - Part Two

In the previous chapter, we started expanding your Git repertoire with 'stash', 'bisect', 'reflog', and 'shortlog'. Now, let's dive even deeper into commands that add precision and customization to your toolkit.

1. "git cherry-pick": Selective Commit Grabbing

Let's say you discover a specific commit on another branch—perhaps a bug fix—that you urgently need in your current branch. Here's how to import it:

```
git cherry-pick <commit_hash>
```

`cherry-pick` carefully transplants the specified commit onto your current branch, creating a new commit with the same changes.

Caution: Cherry-picking rewrites history. Use it judiciously, especially in collaborative projects where the original commit may be part of a shared branch.

2. "git blame": Unveiling the Author of Change

Ever wondered who's responsible for a specific line of code in a legacy project? Behold the power of 'blame':

```
git blame <file_name>
```

This command annotates each line in a file with the commit hash, author, and timestamp of when it was last modified. Perfect for tracing a bug's origin or understanding the historical evolution of a piece of code.

3. "git alias": Customizing Your Shortcuts

Frequent use of long Git commands can become cumbersome. Git aliases allow you to create shortcuts for those complex or regularly used actions:

```
git config --global alias.st status
```

Now, instead of `git status`, you can simply type `git st`. Create as many aliases as you like to streamline your workflow.

Example Aliases

- `git co checkout`
- `git ci commit`
- `git br branch`
- `git unstage reset HEAD`

4. "git config": Personalizing Your Git Experience

Git provides a wealth of configuration options. Use `git config` to customize everything from your username and default editor to advanced behaviors:

- **Setting Your Identity:**

  ```
  git config --global user.name "Your Name"
  git config --global user.email
  "your_email@example.com"
  ```

- **Tweaking Behavior:** Explore the wealth of settings available in the Git documentation.

Additional Resources

- **Git Cherry-Pick Documentation:** https://git-scm.com/docs/git-cherry-pick
- **Git Blame Documentation:** https://git-scm.com/docs/git-blame
- **Git Alias Documentation:** https://git-scm.com/docs/git-alias
- **Git Config Documentation:** https://git-scm.com/docs/git-config

Coming Up...

Well, we are nearing the end! However, it's important to realize the journey of learning Git is a continuous one. There are always new techniques, best practices, and tools to explore. Stay curious, experiment, and embrace the world of online Git resources for continued growth in your version control mastery!

Conclusion

Throughout this book, you've embarked on an extraordinary journey. From the very foundations of Git to the collaborative frontiers of GitHub, you have systematically built a robust understanding of version control concepts and the transformative workflows they enable. Let's recap some of your major milestones:

- **Unleashing Development Superpowers:** You learned to track changes, fearlessly experiment with branches, navigate your project's history with confidence, and recover from missteps with ease.
- **Command Line Confidence:** You've mastered essential Git commands, and even ventured beyond the basics, unlocking tools to enhance your efficiency and precision.
- **Mastering Collaboration:** You now understand how to contribute confidently to projects with pull requests and participate in the code review process, fostering knowledge exchange and improving code quality within teams and the open-source community.
- **Gateway to a Wider World:** GitHub is no longer a mystery. You can create repositories, share your work, collaborate with others, and draw inspiration from a vast network of developers.

Remember, the Journey Continues…

Git mastery is an ongoing process. Here's how to continue your growth:

- **Practice Makes Perfect:** Use Git in your personal projects and seek opportunities to contribute to ones that interest you.
- **Explore Advanced Topics:** Dive deeper into concepts like rebasing, advanced merging strategies, and Git workflows suited to various team structures.
- **Embrace the Community:** Participate in online Git forums and attend local meetups or conferences to connect with fellow developers.

The Power of Version Control

Whether you're a solo developer pursuing side projects or a member of a large development team, the Git and GitHub skills you've gained will transform the way you code. You now have the ability to:

- **Innovate with Less Fear:** Experiment freely, knowing you can always return to a safe state.
- **Build Resilient Projects:** Track code evolution, pinpoint bugs more easily, and recover gracefully from errors.
- **Collaborate Seamlessly:** Contribute to shared codebases with confidence, providing and receiving valuable feedback.

Congratulations! You've equipped yourself with an essential toolset that empowers your coding endeavors, fosters collaboration, and propels you toward continuous improvement. The world of software development awaits, and you're ready to leave your mark!

www.ingramcontent.com/pod-product-compliance
Lightning Source LLC
LaVergne TN
LVHW081804050326
832903LV00027B/2089